HistoryCaps Presents:

The Forgotten League

A History of Negro League Baseball

By Frank Foster

BookCaps™ Study Guides

www.bookcaps.com

FRANK FOSTER

The Forgotten League

Table of Contents

ABOUT HISTORYCAPS

HistoryCaps is an imprint of BookCaps™ Study Guides. With each book, a brief period of history is recapped. We publish a wide array of topics (from baseball and music to science and philosophy), so check our growing catalogue regularly (www.book-caps.com) to see our newest books.

INTRODUCTION

The Negro Leagues have a multifaceted history; just as there was no single inventor of baseball, there is no single origin for the Negro Leagues. It is also necessary to note that the history of the Negro Leagues is not the same as that of black baseball; there was black baseball before the formation of leagues, and the league structure underwent a number of iterations. Because of the incomplete records that were kept, it would be impossible to conduct a comprehensive complete study; in many cases, statistics and anecdotes are apocryphal and many stories have been embellished over time.

Nevertheless, this study represents a basic framework, charting the history of black baseball from the 1860s to the onset of racial integration in Major League Baseball. This examination begins by investigating black baseball before the advent of the Negro Leagues, transitioning into an exploration of the first black teams and professional baseball. Next, the first iteration of the official Negro Leagues and its eventual collapse are discussed, followed by examinations of the heyday of the Negro Leagues in the 1930s until the fall of the color carrier and the dissolution of the Leagues in the postintegration era. Finally, this study concludes by addressing the legacy of black baseball and its contemporary relevance.

CHAPTER 1: THE EARLY DAYS

EARLY BLACK BASEBALL

The earliest recorded baseball games between African-Americans occurred in the wake of the conclusion of the Civil War, not long after the purported advent of white baseball games. Baseball first occurred in the north, mainly in upstate New York (it would be some time before the sport would move into the cities.) Organized baseball began as a truly provincial affair, with large towns and small cities forming teams assembled from local players. There were teams in places like Buffalo, Utica, Rochester, Troy, and Canajoharie. This was the age of the Great Migration and industrial revolution, and baseball was a popular activity for workers during their vacation days.

As the Industrial Revolution progressed, baseball became more urban and was especially popular in New York City. The first documented game took place on November 15, 1859, between the Weeksville Unknowns and the Henson Club of Jamaica (in Queens). The Hensons won 54-43; this score reflects central aspects of the sport in its infant stages; there was mighty little defense, games were lengthy, and a premium was placed on offense. The format and equipment were conducive to high scoring, as the catcher was the only fielder who wore a glove. The game was rough; batters did not wear helmets and catcher's masks were not worn until the 1870s.. Other differences between early and modern-day baseball include that the pitcher was allowed a running start and threw underhand from a box located 45 feet from the plate (in this regard, early baseball was similar to modern-day softball), nine balls were allowed before a walk was issued, the batter dictated where the pitcher was to throw the ball, and flat bats were allowed (a vestige of cricket, a sporting ancestor of baseball.)

Although the first games took place between teams from the same city, after some time teams began traveling to other cities. The first example of this was when the Albany Bachelors went to Philadelphia to play the Excelsiors and Pythians. This and other similar events were sweeping processions and significant events unifying different black communities; there were parties and entertainment productions, and the host team took pride in showing off their city. The teams were not professional, and despite the inherent physical dangers stemming from lack of safety equipment, games were conducted in a spirit of amicable leisure. Baseball quickly emerged as a cultural unifier, and the sport is a useful lens through which to chart a progression from the rural to the urban, and the collective reception associated with watching a baseball game instantly made the game an avatar for modernity in the United States. The combination between the pastoral field and the urban setting made it so that baseball was appeal to uniquely synthesize the rural and the urban at a time when, following the Civil War, the nation was enraptured in conflict between farm and city. Baseball became a leisure activity on par with the carnival and other forms of late 19th century entertainment.

Even before the advent of a league structure, there were team dynasties. Records indicate that the Philadelphia Pythians were the first dominant team, behind the stellar performance of Octavius Catto, who is generally recognized as the first serious star. The Pythians were also known for legitimizing black baseball, exhibiting gentlemanly conduct both on and off the field that helped distance black baseball from the pejorative racial stereotypes of the time. In 1867, the Pythians applied for inclusion into the white National Association of Base Ball Players but were denied acceptance under the despicable rationale that "if colored clubs were admitted there would in all probability be some division of feeling, whereas, by excluding them, no injury could result to anyone." Although this ruling would not entirely prevent black players from playing in the league, it effectively introduced the color barrier since black teams were excluded. As a result, the foundation for the Negro Leagues was born.

EARLY PROFESSIONAL BLACK BASEBALL

The earliest professional black baseball teams played constantly, scheduling a dizzying total of barnstorming exhibition contests. There was no league structure and accordingly, no guaranteed schedule, so teams worked continually at scheduling games. The earliest known black professional team was the Cuban Giants, established in 1885 by Frank P. Thompson. The Giants were an outstanding team, and allegedly won 113 games against just 30 losses in 1887. The team included the legendary George Stovey, as well as stars like Clarence Williams and Abe Harrison. They even played a number of white professional teams, most notably the Cincinnati Reds. They were extremely popular and had two daily newspapers covering the team; perhaps because of this, the Giants were the first team that was widely known. However, despite their popularity, attendance was not satisfactory since the irregular schedule made it difficult for people to commit to attending games well in advance. Additionally, the fact that night baseball had not yet developed also hurt attendance, as many potential fans worked every day and did not have afternoons to spare.

Although black teams were not allowed to play in white leagues, until 1887 there were integrated teams. Bud Fowler was the first African-American to play professionally, and, in 1874, he played for teams located in Worcester and Lynn, Massachusetts. Most notably, in 1884 Moses Walker even played in a professional game, for the Toledo Blue Stockings in the American Association. A catcher, Walker had played for Oberlin College and the University of Michigan. In some ways, he was a 19th century Jackie Robinson, a racial pioneer who was well-educated and had played in college. However, he received broken ribs from pitchers deliberately throwing at him and also received threats via violent and angry letters. Consequently, his plight prevented other teams from hiring black players.

Despite the unfair treatment of blacks, they were still hired to play for certain teams and as many as 3 dozen played during the 1880s. Finally, in 1887 player-manager Cap Anson (a future Hall of Famer) refused to play against Moses Walker's Toledo Blue Stockings. Although no formal rule was enacted, Anson's actions initiated a 'gentleman's agreement' that would prohibit blacks from professional baseball until Jackie Robinson's collapsing of the color barrier 60 years later.

Although African-Americans were forbidden from playing professional baseball, independent league teams continued to hire them. Most notably, the International League, an independent league located in New York state, hired blacks on a regular basis, as Newark, Buffalo, Binghamton, Syracuse, and Oswego all employed blacks. However, they hardly received fair treatment; blacks continued to receive the same prejudiced treatment on the field that they had always been subjected to, intentionally getting hit by pitches and dealing with harassment on a regular basis.

THE EMERGENCE OF TEAMS

The success of the Cuban Giants opened the door for the emergence of more stable teams and a league structure. It quickly became apparent that more money was to be made if the public could rally behind a team from their home town, with regularly scheduled games and identifiable stars. At this time, baseball and organized sport were still in their nascent stages, and the ubiquitous present-day culture of fandom had not been established. Until the end of the 19th century, baseball was more of barnstorming traveling show than an integral aspect of the community. A baseball game was more of an event than a part of people's everyday experiences. Although barnstorming would remain popular, the establishment of leagues was indispensible in popularizing the game to an evergrowing consumer culture. This was the age of urban expansion and black migration northward, as blacks realized that working in cities was more lucrative than conditions in the south. The growth of the Negro Leagues was thus inextricably linked with the improvement of African-American quality of life.

In 1888, teams engaged in a Negro League World Series, with the indomitable Cuban Giants taking on the Pittsburgh Keystones, Norfolk Red Stockings and New York Gorhams. Unsurprisingly, the Giants won, although the grand scale of the event helped grow the sport. As the 1890s arrived, however, black teams began to have difficulty remaining profitable. The economic climate had atrophied to the point that only the wealthiest, most talented teams were able to remain in operation. One of the main reasons for this is that owners were not invested in the welfare of other teams and the league as a whole but rather concentrated on their own teams. Accordingly, there was a competitive and financial imbalance between teams like the Cuban Giants and the rest of the league. However, by the middle of the 1890s, even the Giants experienced financial difficulty and would undergo a number of ownership changes. As a result of the financial troubles that afflicted each of the teams, black baseball began to migrate from east to west, which wound up contributing to the team's demise. The plight of the Cuban Giants elucidates salient aspects of the Negro Leagues; teams did not retain their players, and many lasted for only a short period. Salaries were not generous enough to entice people to stay or engender any loyalty, and players went from team to team on a revolving basis, latching on to whoever was willing to pay the most money.

Despite their struggles, the Cuban Giants had an established name and continued to survive even while other teams were collapsing en masse. Amidst financial trouble, the Cuban Giants were sold to a new owner, who renamed the team the Cuban X Giants. One crucial development, however, involved the formation of the Page Fence Giants, a talented team that finally provided the Cuban Giants with a legitimate rival. The Page Fence Giants became barnstorming legends, touring the Midwest. Led by Bud Fowler, George Wilson, and Billy Holland, the team defeated the Cuban X Giants in a Negro League World Series, with a score of ten games to five. However, the Page Fence Giants collapsed in 1898, and by 1900, the Negro Leagues were in a state of grave financial turmoil.

Following the extinction of the Page Fence Giants, a new team was needed to challenge the Cuban X Giants; this void would be filled by the Philadelphia Giants, who were founded in 1901 and played their first season in 1902. The team was created by Negro League legend Sol White and two sportswriters— H. Walter Schlichter and Harry Smith. From its incipience, the team was enormously talented; new teams in the Negro Leagues were different from modern-day expansion; players were not beholden to their preexisting team and with the right amount of money, they could easily be lured to a new franchise. Accordingly, the Philadelphia Giants immediately recruited catcher Clarence Williams and second baseman Frank Grant. In 1902, they played to a superlative record of 81 wins, 43 losses, and 2 ties (ties were a viable outcome in baseball's early days due to the lack of lighting—games often ended prematurely due to darkness.) The Giants attempted to schedule a Negro League World Series against the Cuban X Giants, but the Cuban X Giants declined. However, they were able to secure a brief exhibition series against the white Major League Philadelphia Athletics, and although they lost both games played, they comported themselves well and admirably represented black baseball.

The year 1901 is not only significant for the emergence of the Philadelphia Giants but also because the white Major League color barrier was threatened. Charlie Grant, a player originally from Cincinnati, who had spent the 1900 season with the Columbia Giants, was working as a bellhop at the Eastland Hotel in Hot Springs, Arkansas in March. This was not unusual; it was quite common for Negro Leaguers (and white Major Leaguers as well) to work alternate jobs in the baseball off-season. One day, famed Baltimore Orioles player-manager John McGraw observed Grant playing a game of baseball with his hotel cohorts. Enraptured, McGraw signed him, attempting to pass of Grant as a Cherokee native-American named Chief Tokahoma. Although McGraw's actions represent racist stereotyping in its own right, it is significant that the color barrier darned nearly was crossed, if not broken. Ultimately, however, the episode came to an end when Charlie Comiskey, the owner of the Chicago White Sox, spotted Grant and forced him out of the game; baseball would then wait another 46 years before integrating.

From 1902-108, the Philadelphia Giants were a considerable dynasty; in 1903, they would lose the colored championship to the Cuban X Giants, but, in 1904, the Giants were able to recruit Rube Foster, arguably the greatest player in baseball and they would win the championship for the next five years. In 1904, their adversary was the Cuban X Giants, and Foster delivered two victories against his former club to take the series two games to one. The following year would see the Philadelphia Giants play a different foe, the Brooklyn Royal Giants, but again the result was the same, as Philadelphia won three games to none.

Baseball is more steeped in tradition than any other American sport, and so it may seem strange that the game changed so drastically from one year to the next around the turn of the century. It is crucial to remember that baseball was much less financially secure than it is today, and there was an element of improvisation that characterized the Negro Leagues. Teams had singularly little continuity, with players skipping from one team to the next on an almost revolving basis (in this regard, the Negro Leagues were somewhat closer to modern-day baseball, with free agency, than to white baseball of the time period), and the situation was to a large degree 'every player for himself.' The team that won the most often was not the team with the smartest owner or general manager, but rather the one with the most money. The career of Rube Foster demonstrates this tendency; from the end of the 19th century through the first decade-plus of the 20th century, whichever team had Rube Foster typically won the championship. There were dynasties in the Negro Leagues, but the league featured a decidedly uneven distribution of talents. The best players were likely as talented as those who have ever played the game, but the lesser players were not as strong as those in the white Major Leagues. Accordingly, there was extremely little competitive balance in the Leagues, as the rich got richer while the poor struggled to survive.

In 1906, the first organized black baseball league was formed, with the title International League of Colored Baseball Clubs in America and Cuba. The league featured six organizations: the Cuban X Giants, Philadelphia Quaker Giants (not the same team as the Philadelphia Giants, the Cuban Stars, the Havana Stars of Cuba, the Philadelphia Professionals, and the Riverton Palmyra. Shortly thereafter, the Philadelphia Giants and Wilmington Giants would replace the Philadelphia Quaker Giants and Cuban Stars, respectively. That year, the Cuban X Giants and Philadelphia Giants would again square off for the championship title, with the Philadelphia Giants winning for the "World's Colored Championship."

In 1907, the Philadelphia Giants would suffer the same fate as the teams that lost players to the Giants; Rube Foster (along with fellow star teammate Pete Hill and a few other teammates) left the team to join the Leland Giants. The Leland Giants were founded in 1905 and were a descendent of the Chicago Union Giants. For their first couple of years, the team had not excelled, but after acquiring an abundance of talent paid the difference for them and they became an instant powerhouse. Of all the lovely seasons in Negro League history, the regular season of the Leland Giants in 1907 was arguably the greatest. They would finish with a record of 110 wins against just 10 loses, with 48 consecutive victories. However, the Philadelphia Giants would again get the better of the competition and win the World's Colored Championship.

In 1908, the Philadelphia Giants and the Leland Giants played each other in the World's Colored Championship once again; the two teams played to a 3-3 tie as a seventh game was never played. Even though the regular season schedules were shorter for Negro League teams than their white counterparts, teams frequently went on prolonged barnstorming tours in the offseason, often traveling south to the Caribbean. In 1907, for example, the Philadelphia Giants toured Cuba, and over the years, exhibitions between Negro League teams and white Major League teams occurred frequently during the off-season.

Over the next couple of years, Rube Foster emerged as the dominant figure in Negro League baseball. A Texan, Foster was raised in a strictly religious household, and his father was a Methodist reverend. His thick physique bore resemblance to Babe Ruth, neither looked like an athlete yet both were innately gifted in the sport. Foster possessed the larger-than-life persona that Ruth would later become known for, and his name became synonymous with black baseball. His colorful antics earned him publicity and a reputation; one of his most famous characteristics was that he always carried a gun on him—even while he was pitching! He had begun his career in 1897 with the Waco Yellow Jackets, and, in 1902, he earned his nickname when he outpitched the white baseball star Rube Waddell in an exhibition game in 1902. Since the first years of the 20th century, he had been arguably the greatest player in the Negro Leagues, but as the decade progressed, he assumed an administrative role in black baseball. In 1910, Foster acquired control of the Leland Giants and became player-manager for the team. Ever the lucrative businessman, he scheduled a more comprehensive, rigorous barnstorming schedule; Foster would later state that the 1910 Leland Giants team was the greatest Negro League ballclub every assembled. The team had not only Foster but also John Henry Lloyd, Bruce Petway, and Pat Dougherty; certainly, Foster had ample evidence proving his claim, as the Giants won an incredible 123 victories against just six losses. Foster even secured an exhibition series against the Chicago Cubs, and although the Leland Giants lost to the defending white Major League champions, the games were close, and Foster's team held leads on multiple occasions. At any rate, the Leland Giants were better than a number of white Major League teams, and it is also beneficial to remember that there were likely many more victories that went undocumented, a product of the notoriously incomplete annals of Negro League history.

1911 was another formative year in Negro League history. Ever the itinerant player-businessman, Rube Foster broke away from the Leland Giants and started the Chicago American Giants. This would have a drastic impact on the landscape of black baseball as it afforded Foster an even more powerful platform with which to market his team—Foster partnered with the wealthy Chicago businessman John M. Schorling and took over the previous ball park of the Chicago White Sox. The South Side location was crucial in marketing the game, as there was a large black population that became drawn to the always-magnetic Foster and his baseball heroics. With the arrival of the Great Migration, blacks moved into the cities and began making enough money to afford moderate expenses like baseball games. Foster knew that baseball players had always been criminally underpaid, and he used his authority to ensure that he received a substantial percentage of the profits. Throughout the decade, he made a generous living, relying on gate receipts and a robust exhibition schedule.

During the second decade of the 20th century black baseball was expanding, but so too was the landscape of the United States. Although a number of players left to fight in World War One, the talents of Rube Foster and his Chicago American Giants made the team perhaps the greatest dynasty in either white or colored baseball. Foster knew that the west coast represented a ripe potential baseball audience, and although the majority of his schedule was located in the Midwest, he began scheduling exhibitions along the west coast. From 1912-1915,

Foster organized a west-coast barnstorming tour in the winter. At this time period, there were no white Major League baseball teams on the west coast, and Foster's off-season barnstorming tours were integral in spreading the sport's popularity to the new demographic.

Throughout the remainder of the decade, black baseball teams continued to operate independently. It was a lucrative business, although it relied on a savvy businessperson like Rube Foster to turn a strong profit (and indeed, Foster made almost $15,000 in 1919), since teams had no stable league structure guaranteeing games. To make matters worse, teams had difficulty promoting games on the east coast and booking stadiums with the independent structure. Ultimately, the success of black baseball necessitated a league structure, similar to that of the white Major Leagues.

CHAPTER 2: FORMATION OF THE NEGRO NATIONAL LEAGUE

After the 1919 season, black baseball was in a state of transition. Team owners realized that they needed more consistency; fans in a city needed to have a home team they could rely on, with more tangible rivalries and identifiable stars. To remedy this, Rube Foster met with the owners of seven other preexisting teams on February 13, 1920 at a YMCA in Kansas City. Foster would not only serve as the player-manager for his Chicago American Giants, but also the owner of the team and the commissioner for the league. The eight founding teams were the Chicago American Giants, Kansas City Monarchs, Chicago Giants, Indianapolis ABCs, Cuban Stars, Dayton Marcos, Detroit Stars, and St. Louis Giants. Each of these teams was located in the Midwest, reflecting the shifting demographics of black baseball.

All of the owners were black with the exception of J.L. Wilkinson, the owner of the Kansas City Monarchs. A failed pitching prospect, Wilkinson had been influential in supporting baseball integration for years. From 1912 to 1920, he had operated the All Nations barnstorming club, a team that featured players from a number of different ethnicities, including white, black, Asian, and Native Americans. In 1909, he had also briefly operated an all-women team. It is no accident that he was the only white owner out of the original eight Negro National League teams; over the course of the previous decade, he had garnered the trust of Rube Foster, who knew that Wilkinson was both racially tolerant and financially successful enough to support the team.

In the league's first year, Foster's Chicago American Giants won the league championship, although the Detroit Stars, Kansas City Monarchs, and Indianapolis ABCs were also quite talented. Although the league structure guaranteed games for teams, the structure was not perfect; clubs continued to

play an uneven number of games, and the Dayton
Marcos were unable to sustain their existence. They
were dropped from the league following the 1920
season replaced by the Columbus Buckeyes. Meanwhile, the Cubans began playing their home games
in Cincinnati.

Although there was finally an official league structure, the barnstorming legacy was never supplanted. In addition to their regular season, teams would
typically barnstorm between 50-150 exhibition contests a year. Accordingly, the regular season was
never more than 100 games, significantly shorter
than the white Major League season. Teams also
controlled their own scheduling; not only did this
lead to a terribly uneven number of games played,
but the clubs were able to control the ratio of
league and exhibition games.

The Chicago American Giants would go on to win
the Negro National League in 1921 and 1922, behind
Rube Foster's model of excellent pitching and defense. The St. Louis Giants were another excellent
team, although it was the Kansas City Monarchs
that emerged as the foremost competition for Foster's ballclub. The two teams would compete head-
to-head for years for the championship title.

The Negro National League was an immediate success. The small number of teams concentrated the

number of games and Foster's careful screening
process had ensured that the owners were responsible and financially capable of running their teams.
Attendance was strong, and the east coast began to
take notice. Until this point, the east coast had been
filled with independent teams, similar to the Midwest before the advent of the Negro National
League. There were, undeniably, many strong teams
in the east, particularly the Bacharach Giants of Atlantic City and the Hilldale Club of Philadelphia.
Both of these teams had been ancillary members of
the Negro National League, although the situation
was not in their best interest since they were prohibited from competing for the championship and
so were not as attractive to potential fans. In 1923, a
group of East coast owners met and founded the
Eastern Colored League. The charter teams were
Hilldale, the Bacharach Giants, Cuban Stars, Brooklyn Royal Giants, New York Lincoln Giants, and the
Baltimore Black Sox. Concentrated in large Northeast cities, the Eastern League was a far more corporate environment than the Negro National
League; the league was tainted with a somewhat
ignoble reputation as some of the owners had made
their fortune from gambling or other ventures of ill
repute. Still, the quality of play was high, and the
Eastern Colored League proved an enduring rival to
their Midwestern counterparts.

1923 was also a significant year because the Kansas City Monarchs finally supplanted Rube Foster's Chicago American Giants as the best team in the Negro National League. During the season, the Monarchs released manager Sam Crawford and hired the former Cuban star Jose Mendez. In addition to his managerial duties, Mendez was a star nearly on par with Rube Foster in his prime, and the team instantly transformed itself into a dynasty. The balance of power was beginning to shift; Foster's club finished in third place, behind not only the Monarchs but also the Detroit Stars. Foster was growing older (by this point, he was well past 40 years of age), and his team was no match for the Monarchs, who had assembled an outstanding roster filled with stars such as future Hall of Famer Bullet Joe Rogan, George Carr, and Rube Currie.

Going into the 1924 season, the Negro Leagues were thriving, both on the East coast and in the Midwest. However, what was lacking was a year-end championship bringing the leagues together in the manner that the white Major Leagues had their World Series championship each fall. To remedy this, the two leagues agreed to stage a "World Championship of Negro Baseball" between the winners of each league. Rube Foster approved this after some deliberation; although no one cared as much as Foster did about the welfare and status of black baseball, he had been reticent to approve the

World Championship. The relations between the two leagues were not especially amicable, largely because the Eastern teams had purchased a number of players from the Negro National League. Moreover, Foster's own Chicago American Giants were no longer the premier team in the Midwest, making it so that his team would not represent the Negro National League in the inaugural series. In the end, however, the series was approved and the Kansas City Monarchs defeated the Hilldale club in a tight series, winning 5 games to 4, with 1 tie. Although the attendance throughout the series was erratic, with crowds ranging from 584 to 8,661 fans, the series was a success and would continue for the next several years.

Also in 1924, the Negro National League expanded its demographic, incorporating two new teams from the Southeast, the Birmingham Black Barons and the Memphis Red Sox. However, Indianapolis collapsed in June and by this time the Chicago Giants had also folded, so there were still 8 teams in each league. That same year, the Eastern Colored League expanded, and two new teams were added, the Harrisburg Giants and the Washington/Wilmington Potomacs.

In 1925, the Monarchs again won the Negro National League; the league was divided into first and second halves, with Kansas City taking the first and

the St. Louis Stars winning the second half. The
Monarchs defeated the Stars in a playoff to decide
who would take on the Eastern League champion,
and the Monarchs won 5 games to 3. The Monarchs
went on to defeat the Hilldales and repeated as Negro World Champions.

The 1926 season is as notable for what happened
off the field as the proceedings on field. Rube Foster, perhaps the greatest figure in Negro League
history, began suffering from dementia, subsumed
in the erroneous belief that he was being called
upon to pitch in the white Major League World Series. He would eventually move into a mental institution in Kankakee, Illinois and would pass away
just four years later, at the premature age of 51.
Eventually, he was elected to the Hall of Fame by
the Veteran's Committee, although it is a travesty
that he was not admitted with the first wave of Negro League greats, who had been elected a decade
earlier.

Despite the trials of their owner, the Chicago
American Giants thrived in 1926 and 1927. Prior to
the season, Rube Foster had forced the Memphis
Red Sox into relinquishing his brother, Bill Foster,
who would become the team's star pitcher. In his
comprehensive history of the Negro Leagues,
Lawrence Hogan refers to 1926 as the heyday of the
Negro Leagues, and indeed the season was filled

with incredible contests. The Monarchs won the first half of the National League season, while the Chicago American Giants took the second half. The Giants defeated Kansas City in a thrilling playoff, 5 games to 4. In the Eastern League, the Bacharach Giants defeated the Harrisburg Senators in another dramatic series. Behind the arm of Bill Foster, the Chicago American Giants then defeated the Bacharach Giants of Atlantic City for the World Series title.

The season was also remarkable for the (short-lived) emergence of a new league located in the South and not affiliated with the National or Eastern leagues. The league consisted of the Birmingham Black Barons and Memphis Red Sox (who had removed themselves from the National League), as well as the Louisville White sox, Albany (Georgia) Giants, Atlanta Black Crackers, Montgomery Gray Sox, and Chattanooga White Sox. The teams played a reasonably robust schedule of over 50 games, and although the league lasted just one year, it was tremendously popular and helped popularize baseball in the Southern United States.

CHAPTER 3: THE BEGINNING OF THE END FOR THE NEGRO LEAGUES OF THE 1920S

If 1926 was one of the most successful seasons in Negro League history, the following year was one of the most problematic. Financial woes befell the teams; the Eastern Colored League was affected most quickly, and the Atlantic City Bacharach Giants—always one of the best teams in black baseball—went bankrupt after the season ended. The National League was not doing well either, and

Rube Foster's absence was sorely missed. To fill his shoes, William C. Hueston, a judge, was hired as league commissioner. However, while Hueston was a terrific legislator, he lacked Foster's baseball acumen and business sense. Players went barnstorming in Japan and without a strong spokesperson for the league, the players' lack of commitment to the league—always perhaps the greatest limitation affecting black baseball—became exposed.

That season, the Chicago American Giants won the National League, with a record of 32-14. In the league playoff series, the Giants beat the Birmingham Black Barons. In the Eastern League, the Bacharach Giants were league champions. In the World Series, the Chicago American Giants defeated the Bacharach Giant, 5 games to 3. Although his team would eventually lose the World Series, it was notable for the fact that Luther Farrell, a pitcher for the Bacharach Giants, threw a no hitter in one of the games.

Even though 1927 was a terrible year for the Negro Leagues as a whole, there were exciting developments. The season saw the emergence of future Hall of Famer Turkey Stearns, and Satchel Paige had his rookie season for the Birmingham Black Barons, who were reinstated back into the league along with a team from Memphis.

Satchel Paige would go on to have arguably the greatest career of anyone in Negro League history, and his life story reads as though it were constructed by a gifted storyteller. He grew up in abject poverty and learned baseball while in a child correctional institution. He was born the seventh of eleven children, and his father was a gardener while his mother was a washerwoman. Paige had trouble with the law growing up, and the reform school to which he was assigned, the Industrial School for Negro Children (located in Mount Meigs, Alabama) would provide him with the structure needed to develop as a ballplayer and as a man. It gave him a place to stay and kept him fed, and there was a baseball team. The baseball coach there nurtured his talent and gave him the framework he would use to dominate hitters for the next 20 years.

Paige's first professional baseball contract was with the Chattanooga Black Lookouts of the Southern Negro League for $200 a month, but he broke the contract after the New Orleans Pelicans offered him a car to pitch for them. This episode was representative of Paige's sensibility; he was undeniably talented, but always looked out for his own best interests and was notorious for moving from one team to the next, even when he was under contract with another team. He was an independent entity who played for whoever would pay him the most money. Paige was a master showman and delighted in entertaining people with creative nicknames for his pitches. These included (there may well have been many more) the bee ball, the jump ball, the trouble ball, Long Tom, Little Tom, midnight rider, four-day creeper, and hesitation pitch. He became a true fan favorite, delighting fans with his showmanship. In one famous maneuver, he would announce that he would strike out the first nine batters and call the infield in; another famous stunt was to walk the bases loaded, tell his fielders to lie down, and then strike out the side. Satchel loved attention, and he often arrived late for games and reveled in the grand entrance he received. Antics aside, Satchel Paige was one of the greatest pitchers of all time and almost certainly the best to ever pitch in the Negro Leagues. No player was in greater demand, and the scope of his popularity was perhaps greater than any single player in the white Major Leagues save for Babe Ruth. The larger-than-life personas of players like Paige and Rub Foster demonstrates how what the Negro Leagues may have lacked in depth of talent it recuperated through its star power.

By 1927, with the popularity of the Negro Leagues beginning to wane, the independently-operated Homestead Grays remained popular. The Grays were founded in 1912 by Cumberland Posey, a wealthy businessman; the team was located in Pittsburgh and played many of their home games at

Forbes Field, the stadium for the Pittsburgh Pirates, the white Major League team located in Pittsburgh. They were not part of the Negro Leagues but nevertheless played a rigorous barnstorming schedule, remaining among the most popular franchises in black baseball. Posey had a strong affiliation with the *Pittsburgh Courier*, an influential African-American newspaper. His team remained financially secure, as Posey had the financial resources to attract premium talent and was not ashamed to raid the talent of the Negro League rosters. In 1925, he signed Smokey Joe Williams, who became one of the greatest Negro League pitchers of all time, and 1927 saw the arrival of Cuban superstar Martin Dihigo. They also had star shortstop Bobby Williams and slugger John Beckwith. In the end, more than half of the Negro Leaguers in the Hall of Fame played for the Homestead Grays at one period or another. The success of the Grays serves as another example of the economics of the Negro Leagues, in which the rich teams remained profitable while the poor collapsed.

Because Posey often signed Negro League players, he had never gotten along with the league owners. However, by 1928 the Negro Leagues were in a state of financial turmoil, and an alliance between the Grays and the Eastern League developed. The Grays joined the league for the 1928 season, although it would collapse later that season, returning to its former independent structure. Before the season had started, Hilldale, Harrisburg, and the Brooklyn Royal Giants had all withdrawn, and the season was doomed from the start. The Negro National League also collapsed in 1928, a victim of the atrophying of the economic climate. One also cannot ignore the impact that the departure of Rube Foster had made on the league.

Ultimately, the demise of both leagues was the result of a number of factors, mainly relating to the way in which the players and teams were marketed and documented. Because players had no allegiance to their teams, they left with no notice, making it difficult for fans to attach themselves to a given player. Moreover, box scores and statistics were often not reported, so fans had little idea what the standings or league leaders were at any given moment. When results were documented in the papers, there were often conflicting results from one paper to the next.

In 1929, the Negro Leagues restarted with a new concept. There was an American and a National League; the American League consisted of five of the original Eastern Colored League teams, as well as the Homestead Grays. This league never acquired popularity and lasted just one year. The future grew increasingly grim, as only the Homestead Grays remained reasonably profitable. Despite the ill fate of the league, one noteworthy development occurred: the arrival of Josh Gibson, arguably the greatest Negro Leaguer to ever play the game. Gibson was born the son of a sharecropper in Buena Vista, Georgia, and then moved north to Pittsburgh when his father secured a job in a steel mill. He was primed to be an electrician until he realized that baseball would be more lucrative. A strong, thickly-built catcher, he was a progenitor to Major League players like Roy Campanella and Johnny Bench, although Gibson is considered by many to actually be their superior. He is considered the greatest power hitter in Negro League history, and in 1943 hit for an astounding batting average of .517. In his *Historical Baseball Abstract*, Bill James ranks Gibson as the best Negro League player in 1934, 1936, 1938, and 1942-1943. In 1931, playing for the independently-affiliated Grays, Josh hit over 70 home runs; it is alleged that he may have hit as many as 1000 over his career. Gibson's story parallels that of many Negro Leaguers, as black baseball was inextricably linked with the Great Migration and the improving social conditions of the African-American. Indeed, blacks realized that, by moving north, they could improve their fate and make a name for themselves, and baseball was perhaps the most lucrative avenue to explore.

After 1930, the Negro Leagues once again became a barnstorming league. This was a bit archaic, although teams still managed to schedule a large number of contests. The financially affluent Homestead Grays dominated this environment, winning 136 games and just 10 losses in 1931. The barnstorming environment still produced some serious innovations, such as the advent of night baseball. Five years before the purported advent of night baseball, the Kansas City Monarchs invested in a generator and played night games. Their 250 horsepower generator may have been a bit underpowered, and fly balls were virtually guaranteed to fall for extra base hits. This made the games quite lengthy, and players became exhausted as the lighting had allowed the Monarchs to schedule up to three games a day. However, black baseball suffered from the absence of a major league structure; it looked unorganized and less professional than white baseball, and it would only be a matter of time before the leagues were resurrected once again.

CHAPTER 4: THE RETURN OF THE NEGRO LEAGUES

As the 1930s progressed and the economy improved, the climate became suitable for Negro League baseball. In 1931, Gus Greenlee, a Pittsburgh businessman who built his fortune from the gambling enterprise, purchased the Pittsburgh Crawfords baseball club. Greenlee was something of a shady character off the field, and had made a fortune during Prohibition by stealing automobiles filled with beer. After the conclusion of Prohibition, he altered his focus to the gambling market and ran a series of nightclubs and other ventures. He constructed Greenlee field, a grand ballpark that cost $100,000 and represented the premier Negro League stadium, eclipsing the stadium Rube Foster had used for his Chicago American Giants. Always the enterprising individual, Greenlee rented the stadium out for boxing and football events as well, among other purposes. He wasted little time in flexing his financial muscles and in 1932, bought out many of the players from the Homestead Grays, including Josh Gibson, Judy Johnson, and Cool Papa Bell. The famed Oscar Charleston was hired as team manager, and, from the start, the club became a veritable dynasty. The Crawfords also reintroduced a sense of professionalism that had been sorely lacking during the troublesome preceding years; the team comported themselves with ample class, traveling in Lincoln Limousines and booking ballparks in advance. Greenlee also paid his team better than the competition, supplying them with a per diem allowance of $1.50, in addition to their salary.

In 1933, Greenlee, recognizing the necessity for a league structure similar to that of the white Major Leagues, launched the second iteration of the Negro National League. Although it shared the same name, the new National League was, in fact, more similar to the late Eastern Colored League since, for the most part, the teams were located in the East. There were seven teams in total: the Pittsburgh

Crawfords, Homestead Grays, Indianapolis Ameri-
can Giants, Detroit Stars, Baltimore Black Sox,
Nashville Elite Giants, Akron Black Tyrites, Chicago
American Giants (playing under the new title
"Cole's American Giants), and Columbus Blue
Birds. In the inaugural season, the Cole's American
Giants and the Pittsburgh Crawfords tied for the
pennant, but, in a controversial move, the title was
awarded to the Crawfords, perhaps due to the in-
fluence of Gus Greenlee.

More significant than the pennant race was the establishment of a Negro League all-star game,
known as the East-West Classic. The contest occurred in the middle of the season, similar to the
white Major League All-Star Game. It was organized by Gus Greenlee, and the 1933 contest took
place at Comiskey Park, in Chicago. The event was
an enormous success and included players such as
Cool Pappa Bell, Oscar Charleston, Bill Foster, Josh
Gibson, Judy Johnson, Willie Wells, and Turkey
Stearns, and Bill Foster recorded the win. The most
popular event of the season, the East-West classic
would last roughly until the dissemination of the
Negro Leagues in 1950. It would take place in many
of the major cities, such as Chicago, New York,
Washington, D.C., and Cleveland, and was an integral venue in capturing the national spotlight. For
example, the country took notice of Josh Gibson in
1934 after he launched a home run clear out of Yan-

kee Stadium. In many ways, the East-West classic is similar to the All-Star games of today, as players were elected by the fans using ballots published by black newspapers. Fans embraced the proceedings and over the years, it was not unusual for millions of ballots to be cast.

In 1934, the Philadelphia Stars defeated the Chicago American Giants for the pennant, although, in 1935 and 1936, the Pittsburgh Crawfords won both years. The 1935 season saw the arrival of the New York Cubans, who were led by Martin Dihigo and finished as the runner-ups, darned nearly defeating the Crawfords. Ultimately, Pittsburgh was too tough, as Josh Gibson had entered the prime of his career; he would lead the league in home runs in 1932, 1935, and 1936. Unfortunately, many teams were unable to remain profitable, and teams like the Columbus Blue Birds and the Baltimore Black Sox collapsed. Player allegiance was an additional problem; near the end of the 1934 season, Satchel Paige left the Pittsburgh Crawfords to play for a semipro team in North Dakota. He would miss the 1935 season altogether; while it is unfortunate that he chose not to honor his salary and held such little regard for the welfare of the league, Negro League salaries were meager and by signing with the team that offered him the most money, he acted no differently from the majority of modern-day free agents.

Player commitment was an issue that would continue to plague the Negro Leagues for the next several years. Not only was Satchel Paige unpredictable, but in 1937, a number of Pittsburgh Crawford players left for the Caribbean, where the pay was greater and the social conditions vastly superior. Owner Gus Greenlee, noted for his ventures in the gambling industry, ran into trouble with the law after his illegal payments were revealed to the police. Before the season had started, he traded his best player, Josh Gibson, to the Homestead Grays. A famous quote by Willie Wells (while in the Mexican League) sums up the appeal of leaving the United States: "I am not faced with the racial problem...I've found freedom and democracy here, something I never found in the United States. Here in Mexico, I am a man." Leaving the country thus constituted a superior resettlement than the famous Great Migration that had seen black relocate northward in the preceding decades.

In the spring of 1937, Satchel Paige was asked by officials associated with Dominican dictator Rafael Trujillo to play for Los Dragones de Ciudad Trujillo, the team representing the dictator. Paige then recruited Cool Papa Bell and a group of other Negro Leaguers, most notably Josh Gibson. All in all, the group of eight Negro Leaguers split $30,000 for six weeks of playing in the Dominican Republic. The Negro Leaguers enjoyed their time in the Dominican Republic and were well-liked by the fans. They were a fun-loving group, perhaps excessively so; Satchel Paige was a true free spirit and Josh Gibson developed an alcohol addiction as his career progressed. With a .437 batting average, Gibson led the league in batting. However, their team was pressured to win, and the players were even placed in jail before significant contests in order to ensure that they would not carouse too heavily. Although they had enjoyed their time in the city of Santo Domingo, the players were eager to return due to the extreme pressure.

After the brief Dominican League season, Satchel Paige, Cool Papa Bell, and a group of other Negro Leaguers barnstormed rather than returning to the league for the remainder of the season. They performed quite well and went to Denver, where they won a barnstorming competition. Barnstorming success was nothing new to Satchel, as he was famous for Satchel Paige's All-Stars, a barnstorming team that performed successfully against white exhibition teams featuring future Hall of Famers such as Bob Feller, Harry Heilmann, and Dizzy Dean. In fact, arguably Paige's greatest legacy lay on the barnstorming circuit, demonstrating the varied manifestations of black baseball.

The Pittsburgh Crawfords would never return to glory; Gibson was gone forever, as the grade had made him a member of the Homestead Grays once again. In 1939, they left Pittsburgh for Indianapolis, and a year later collapsed as an organization. With the fall of the team, the Homestead Grays returned to prominence, and perhaps the greatest Negro League dynasty of all time was born. Not only did they have Josh Gibson, but they also had an all-time thrilling first baseman in Buck Leonard, who had been with the team since 1934. Indeed, he and Gibson were known as the Babe Ruth and Lou Gehrig of the Negro Leagues, and they would lead the Grays to nine National League Pennants in a row, winning from 1937-1945.

The 1937 season was also remarkable for the establishment of a new Negro League, the Negro American League. Centered in the Midwest, the American League was analogous to the former Negro National League, with the Kansas City Monarchs (still owned by J.L. Wilkinson, Birmingham Black Barons, Chicago American Giants, Cincinnati Tigers, Detroit Stars, Indianapolis Athletics, Memphis Red Sox, and St. Louis Stars. In the inaugural season, the Kansas City Monarchs were league champions, and they would win the league from 1939-1942, with the exception of 1938, when the Memphis Red Sox were champions (some accounts indicate that the Birmingham Black Barons won in 1941 although there is no definitive answer.) According to star player Buck O'Neil, the Monarchs were truly indomitable: "In our baseball, the Kansas City Monarchs were like the New York Yankees in Major League Baseball. Very tops. We had the stars and...we showed it to the world." Not only were they supremely talented, but the Monarchs also had a strong association with the community—the sort of close bond that white Major League teams enjoyed but that the Negro League teams, due to the itinerant players and constantly evolving league structure, had struggled to attain. In 1939, J.L. Wilkinson lured Satchel Paige over to the Monarchs; by this point, Satchel was growing old (in baseball years) and his arm was sore from years of overuse. However, Wilkinson eased him back, and his velocity and pinpoint control returned. In 1941, after two years of rehabilitation, Paige returned to the Monarchs and helped them win the pennant.

By 1942, both Negro Leagues were thriving. There were two dynasties—the Grays in the National League, the Monarchs in the American League—and a midseason All-Star game featuring the best players from each league. However, what was lacking was a world series. For years, the white Major Leagues staged a World Series at the end of the season, with the winners of each league squaring off, and, in 1942, the two Negro Leagues initiated a World Series. This was especially appealing as it would finally feature the Monarchs and Grays squaring off against each other in an official context. The games were played in five different cities, and one of the games did not count, discarded due to protest. The Monarchs won the series easily, sweeping the Grays in four consecutive games.

In 1943, the Homestead Grays again won the pennant and defeated the Birminham Black Barons, 4 games to 3. By this time, the Grays had expanded and included Washington, D.C. as an additional home base. They were enormously popular in the nation's capital and actually featured greater attendance than the white Major League team in Washington, the Senators.

1943 was also significant in that it nearly saw the end of the baseball color barrier. Bill Veeck, the iconoclastic future owner of the Chicago White Sox, St. Louis Browns and Cleveland Indians approached the Philadelphia Phillies and Major League Baseball commissioner Kennesaw "Mountain" Landis in order to purchase the team. However, Landis vetoed the purchase under the auspices that the team was to be operated by the National League until a proper owner was found. Veeck, who had owned the Milwaukee Brewers in the Minor Leagues, had planned to fill the Phillies' roster with Negro League stars. He would have been an enthralling owner to break the color barrier; his humanism was unquestioned, although he was often criticized for what were perceived as publicity stints. During his later ownership ventures, he organized a disco demolition night with the Chicago White Sox in the 1970s, and had sent a three-foot player to bat for the Cleveland Indians. There is the danger that Veeck would have framed baseball integration as a publicity stunt, although one cannot disregard the competitive advantage that was to be gained for the first team with the courage to integrate. It is ironic that the Phillies were so close to being the first team to integrate, since they would eventually become the last team in the National League to sign a black player, waiting until 1957.

By 1944, World War 2 began taking its toll on the Negro Leagues. The War had affected white baseball years earlier, with stars such as Ted Williams and Joe DiMaggio enlisting, but many Negro League stars were over 30 and exempt from service. However, the Negro Leagues would eventually become profoundly affected by the war and notable stars (and future white Major Leaguers) such as Monte Irvin, Larry Doby, Hank Thompson all fought in the war. Altogether, nearly 100 players would serve in the war. World War 2 did have the unintended consequence of strengthening the dominance of the Homestead Grays. Josh Gibson and Buck Leonard, the team's two best players, were exempt from service. Consequently, the Grays beat the Birmingham Black Barons in an easy World Series, 4 games to 1. The Kansas City Monarchs were hit especially hard by the war, as Buck O'Neil, perhaps their best player, had joined the armed services.

In 1945, the Homestead Grays featured an aging roster, but this actually represented a benefit since their players were exempt from the service. By this time, Josh Gibson was 34 years old; meanwhile, Buck Leonard was 38 and Cool Papa Bell was at least 40 (other sources list him as two years older.) They each turned in quality seasons, with Cool Papa Bell especially effective; records indicate that he hit .380 In the World Series, the Grays played against the Cleveland Buckeyes, who had taken advantage of the Kansas City Monarchs' attrition and run away with the Negro American League pennant. Cleveland swept the Grays in four straight games, holding them to three runs over the entire series.

CHAPTER 5: JACKIE ROBINSON AND BASEBALL INTEGRATION

The most significant development in the 1945 season did not involve the Homestead Grays or the Cleveland Buckeyes. Rather, the season will always be remembered for the year in which Jackie Robinson broke into professional baseball. Robinson first became famous after setting national records in track and field. He had also made headlines for his time in the army, during which he refused to move to the back of a bus in the military base. Robinson was honorably discharged for the incident and signed with the Kansas City Monarchs afterwards. Although the Monarchs did not have a terrific year, Robinson had a terrific season for them, batting . 387 and reclaiming his skills after having not played organized baseball in years. He played shortstop and immediately became one of the best players in the league.

Robinson's newspaper connections were indispensable in providing him with the opportunity to break the color barrier. In April of 1945, the mayor of Boston organized for three African-American players to try out for the Boston Red Sox and *Pittsburgh Courier* reporter Wendell Smith selected the individuals. Smith was a close friend of Jackie's and Robinson, along with two other black players (Sam Jethroe and Marvin Williams) tried out for the Red Sox at Fenway Park on April 16. The affair was much publicized, particularly in the African-American press, although the Red Sox had no intention of actually hiring the players and the episode was a mere attempt to appease the Boston mayor.

The tryout with the Red Sox was a serious disappointment, a patronizing event that was dispiriting not only to Robinson but also black baseball as a whole. However, in August of the same year, while Jackie was rehabilitating an injury, Brooklyn Dodgers scout Clyde Sukeforth visited Robinson, on assignment from Branch Rickey, the Dodgers' general manager. After getting to know Jackie, Sukeforth transported him to meet with Branch Rickey—as Jackie was injured, this was acceptable since he was not missing any games. Jackie's appointment with Branch Rickey occurred on August 28, and the meeting lasted a full three hours. Branch Rickey was an innovative owner, a precursor to Bill Veeck, who was constantly experimenting with new methods that might give him a competitive advantage over the competition. While with the St. Louis Browns in the 1930s he had developed the farm team structure, in which the minor leagues were subsidiaries of a parent Major League team. Also similar to Veeck, Rickey had a deep commitment to social justice and racial equality.

Signing Negro League baseball players also represented an additional possible avenue with which to gain an edge on the competition. The Brooklyn Dodgers had been terrible for years, and in the years before free agency, one could not simply buy expensive players on the open market to solve a team's deficiencies. Signing black players held considerable potential, and with the passing of Commissioner Landis a few years prior, the Dodgers General Manager obtained the approval of Landis' successor, "Happy" Chandler. Rickey asked Jackie a number of questions; he needed to hire someone who would not lie down in the face of extreme prejudice. However, he also needed a player who was even-tempered enough not to fight back with violence. Over the years, Jackie had incurred a reputation for being a bit hot-tempered, and Rickey needed to be sure that he could keep his emotions moderated. Jackie impressed him with his sharp mind and assertive demeanor, and an agreement was reached for Jackie to sign with the Dodgers after the conclusion of the season. On October 23, 1945, Jackie signed a minor league contract to play with the Dodgers' minor-league affiliate (the Montreal Royals) for the 1946 season. If all went well, he would join the big-league club in 1947.

It is intriguing to speculate as to exactly why it was Jackie who was chosen to break the color barrier. He was certainly not the most famous black baseball player—that honor would go to Satchel Paige or Cool Papa Bell—but Robinson possessed several unique attributes. First, he had been to college; although he left UCLA one year before graduating, he was a renowned multisport athlete who articulated himself intelligently. Second, Robinson had been around whites his entire life. He grew up a predominantly white neighborhood in Pasadena, California, and had been forced to endure racial prejudice and coexist with whites while in school and the military. Third, Jackie held a serious, focused disposition and a deep investment in civil rights. While players such as Satchel Paige and Buck O'Neil were committed to African-American rights, Paige's showboat antics might have been construed as representative of the pejorative caricature of the black 'song and dance man.' All in all, Robinson best satisfied the criteria Rickey was searching for in choosing the man who would end baseball's 60-year unofficial ban on baseball integration.

CHAPTER 6: THE POST-INTEGRATION NEGRO LEAGUES

Even though baseball integration had been anticipated for years, many Negro League owners and players did not accept the development with enthusiasm. Although he was a civil rights advocate, Kansas City Monarchs owner J.L. Wilkinson was upset since he had Robinson under contract for one more season, and Jackie was likely the team's best player. Other Negro League personalities were more vociferous: Cum Posey referred to Branch Rickey as a "their and robber" after one of their pitchers was subsequently signed by Rickey. Owners were losing their star players one after another and receiving no remuneration. For most of the Negro League owners, their baseball teams had never been a source of considerable profit, but losing their best players left them financially handicapped beyond repair.

Perhaps surprisingly, many players were unhappy about the implementation of integration. Although the plight of the ballplayers that were signed by white Major League teams improved dramatically, lesser players lost their jobs as teams folded. The white Major League teams only signed star Negro Leaguers, and so the less-talented players often had no team for which to play. While it is true that the Negro Leagues would survive for several years after Jackie Robinson was signed by the Dodgers, teams began collapsing. The 1948 season would be the last for the Negro National League, and although versions of the Negro American League would continue for a number of years, profits became quite meager. In 1950, the Chicago American Giants folded, and, in 1951, the Homestead Grays followed suit. The Negro Leagues were negatively affected by the extraordinarily slow pace of integration, as well. Many players were eventually signed by white Major League clubs, but they were forced to toil for years while the Major Leagues completed the transition. Moreover, the fact that Negro League teams were, with few exceptions, located in the same cities as Major League clubs hurt their fate. Consequently, the few teams that managed to survive were for the most part located in cities that did not have Major League teams, such as Indianapolis and Birmingham.

It was not only racial integration that hurt the Negro Leagues. The emergence of television made it so that people did not attend games with their prior frequency. Since Negro League games were not shown on television, they did not benefit from the technological innovation. At the same time, television played a formidable role in baseball integration since the white Major League teams were forced to search for innovative ways of drawing fans. Integration was not only an attraction to white audiences but also tapped into the black market. Sure enough, in 1947 the Dodgers' attendance numbers increased, and when the Cleveland Indians integrated in 1948, their attendance increased by a full 50%. While it is true that attendance fluctuates from one season to the next and the Dodgers and Indians were in the process of luring fans returning from the war, baseball integration was an influential measure in ensuring that baseball remained the country's foremost sporting attraction.

After baseball integration, the remaining Negro Leagues functioned analogously to an independently operated minor league team that prepared players to get drafted by Major League teams. Larry Doby, star player for the Newark Eagles, was signed by Bill Veeck in 1947 (now the owner of the Cleveland Indians in the American League) and became the first black player to play in the American League when he debuted in 1948. Other black players who made an immediate impact were Don Newcombe, Sam Jethroe, Willie Mays, Joe Black, Junior Gilliam, Frank Robinson, Orlando Cepeda, Willie McCovey, and Billy Williams; each would win the Rookie of the Year award for their respective league, as would Jackie Robinson himself in 1947. Hank Aaron, owner of the second-most home runs in baseball history, played in the Negro Leagues before being signed by the Braves, and legendary Chicago Cubs shortstop Ernie Banks had Negro League experience. In many cases, these players dominated the Major Leagues, and their success testifies to the strong player development and high standard of play in the Negro Leagues.

African-American players made an immediate impact, and their legacy is reflected in the annals of the Hall of Fame. Although the incomplete records kept (particularly in the early days of black baseball) have resulted in many of the players being forgotten, there are still 35 individuals who either played in the Negro Leagues or were associated with them (such as J.L. Wilkinson and Cumberland Posey.)

Jackie Robinson became the first black player inducted in the Hall of Fame in 1962, and a Veteran's Committee was established to identify many of the players. Roy Campanella, the famous Brooklyn Dodgers catcher and teammate of Jackie Robinson, was honored in 1969. Following Campanella's induction, the Veteran's Committee inducted one Negro League player for each position: the 'charter' members were Josh Gibson (catcher), Satchel Paige (pitcher), Buck Leonard (first base), Martin Dihigo (second base), John Henry Lloyd (shortstop), Judy Johnson (third base), and Cool Papa Bell, Oscar Charleston, and Monte Irvin in the outfield. Rube Foster had to wait until 1981 to receive his recognition, while his brother Bill was inducted in 1996. Other inductees included Bullet Joe Rogan, Smokey Joe Williams, Willie Wells, and Turkey Stearns. Sam Lacy and Wendell Smith, the famous reporter for the *Pittsburgh Courier*, were inducted for their pioneering work in the media.

CONCLUSION

Given the obstacles faced, it is remarkable that the Negro Leagues were able to survive as long as they did. Given that so many of the teams were owned by African-Americans, securing bank loans was a difficult proposition. Playing conditions were, for the most part, terrible, and players truly played for love of the game. In a famous quote, Satchel Paige stated that "we were worked like the mule that plows the fields all week and drives the carriage to church on Sunday." There was no spring training period for players to ease back into playing conditions. Because rosters typically consisted of just fourteen to sixteen players (roughly ten fewer than

the white Major Leagues) players were often forced
to play through injury. Conditions were terrible and
teams were often relegated to playing in sandlots
and meadows rather than in elaborate stadiums.

Despite the unfortunate positions, the Negro
Leagues were ingenious in their player development. The invention of the minor league system is
now attributed to the Negro Leagues, as the Kansas
City Monarchs had a farm team many years before
Branch Rickey adopted the structure. The very fact
that former Negro Leaguers were able to instantly
dominate Major League baseball testifies to the
high level of play in black baseball and their superlative ability to develop talent.

The Negro Leagues should not only be remembered for the players who integrated into white
baseball. Black baseball should also be commemorated for popularizing a unique style of baseball
different from that of white baseball. Indeed, black
baseball featured a more daring playing style; the
walk was denigrated and players were encouraged
to steal bases as much as possible—legend has it
that Cool Papa Bell once went from first to third
base on a bunt. While they played with considerable focus, black players were also highly aware of
the need to engage fans, and they viewed themselves as entertainers. Accordingly, Negro Leaguers
delighted in devising entertaining nicknames that

endeared them to the fans, and colorful monikers were more popular than among their white counterparts. Examples of such nicknames include "Bullet" Joe Rogan, "Smokey" Joe Wood, and "Double Duty" Radcliffe. The audacious playing style and whimsical tenor reflected a playful spirit more pronounced than that of white baseball.

Given the immediate impact that African-American players brought to the Major Leagues, it is strange that baseball was so slow to fully integrate. Research has shown that teams that hired black players won more often, with one study finding that every black player brought a team an additional six wins in 1950. Certainly, this state is due in large part to the fact that Major League teams only signed black superstars at first, but the impact is still remarkable. The National League integrated far more rapidly than the American League. Even after the color barrier was broken, the American League lagged behind the National League in terms of hiring African-Americans until the 1970s. On average, American League teams hired roughly five fewer African-Americans than National League teams. Much of this is due to the hegemony of the American League, particularly the New York Yankees. For years, the Yankees were the standard-bearers for the American League, and they were highly resistant to hire black players, waiting until 1954 with the signing of catcher (and former Kansas City

Monarch) Elston Howard. It has been asserted that even after integrating, the Yankees were prejudiced against signing African-Americans, and indeed they signed exceedingly few even through the 1960s. An additional explanation for the dilatory pace of American League integration is that American League owners (with a few exceptions, such as Bill Veeck of the Cleveland Indians) were more racist than National League owners. While this is obviously difficult to prove definitively, it is true that owners such as the Red Sox's Tom Yawkey openly condemned the inclusion of African-Americans in Major League Baseball. Not only were the Red Sox the last team to sign a black player (they finally signed Pumpsie Green in 1959), but they did not have a black player regularly in their starting lineup until the 1960s.

Although the Yankees would continue to enjoy success throughout the 1950s and into the 1960s, the National League tilted the balance in power, in large part due to the increased number of African-American players. By 1963, the Yankees' decades-long period of dominance had ended, and they would struggle to remain relevant for the next dozen years. From 1963 until 1982, the National League won 19 out of 20 contests. Teams like the Giants, Dodgers, and Braves collected World Series titles after prolonged droughts. It is clear that hiring blacks represented a competitive balance that perfectly transformed the competitive landscape of Major League Baseball.

Ultimately, the Negro Leagues cannot be commemorated in the same manner as the white Major Leagues. One of the appeals to Major League history is the emphasis placed on statistics. Even though the specific statistics that are favored have evolved over time, baseball has always placed a greater emphasis on statistics than other sports. Even the casual baseball fan knows that Joe DiMaggio once had a 56-game hitting streak, that Barry Bonds hit 73 home runs in a season and that Cy Young won 511 games. However, Negro League history does not lend itself to this type of commemoration; statistics are unreliable and incomplete. Moreover, teams often played as many or more exhibition contests than league games. Noted statistician Bill James has gone so far as to say that "The leagues were the yolk of the egg, the nucleus of a world that extended from the Dominican Republic to Alberta, from the ice up north to the equator and below and included dozens of other leagues, organized at various times." While it is entertaining to ruminate on the stats that have been recorded, it is a reductive exercise conditions were not uniform between teams or from one year to the next.

The most productive lens by which to examine the Negro Leagues is as a rubric enables one to examine the improving conditions of the African-American race. Baseball played a significant role in the urbanization of African-Americans. According to Bill James, the game was played in at least 27 cities: Atlanta, Atlantic City, Baltimore, Birmingham, Brooklyn, Chicago, Cincinnati, Cleveland, Columbus, Dayton, Detroit, Harrisburg, Houston, Indianapolis, Jacksonville, Kansas City, Louisville, Memphis, Milwaukee, Nashville, New York, Newark, Philadelphia, Pittsburgh, St. Louis, Toledo, and Washington, D.C. Very few of these teams were located in the Jim Crow south, and black baseball reflects the black migration away from the deep south and into northern industrial cities. While the majority of Negro League players were born in the south, baseball allowed them the opportunity to improve their conditions.

Today, baseball has been supplanted by basketball and football with regard to popularity among African-Americans. However, perhaps the greatest legacy of black baseball and the end of segregated baseball is that it transformed Major League Baseball into a global game. Not only were African-Americans allowed to play, but Hispanics such as Roberto Clemente were admitted. Currently, the percentage of blacks in Major League Baseball is quite small compared to three or four decades ago as baseball has significantly more whites and Hispanics, as well as players of Japanese and Chinese descent. Nevertheless, baseball proved that African-Americans could play professional sports at a world-class level, and indeed the baseball record books attest to the achievements of black players. It is imperative that the history of black baseball be honored, not only for their significance within their contemporary moment but also because of the influence that the black athletic pioneers had on Major League Baseball and the condition of the African-American race.

BIBLIOGRAPHY

Baseball-Reference. 2000-2012. 18-21 Aug 2012.

Burns, Geoffrey C., and Ken Burns. *Baseball: An Illustrated History.* New York: Alfred Knopf, 1994.

Cottrell, Robert C. *The Best Pitcher in Baseball: The Life of Rube Foster, Negro League Giant.* New York: NYU Press, 2001.

Goff, Brian L. et al. "Racial Integration as an Innovation: Empirical Evidence from Sports Leagues" *The American Economic Review* 92.1 (Mar. 2002): 16-26.

Gudmestad, Robert H. "Baseball, the Lost Cause, and the New South in Richmond, Virginia, 1883-1890" *The Virginia Magazine of History and Biography* 106.3 (Summer 1998): 267-300.

Hanssen, Andrew. "The Cost of Discrimination: A Study of Major League Baseball," *Southern Economic Journal* 64.3 (Jan. 1998): 603-627.

Hogan, Lawrence D., and Jules Tygiel. *Shades of Glory: The Negro Leagues and the Story of African-American Baseball.* Washington: National Geographic Publishing, 2006.

James, Bill. *The New Bill James Historical Baseball Abstract.* New York: Simon and Schuster, 2001.

Stout, Glenn. "Tryout and Fallout: Race, Jackie Robinson, and the Red Sox," *Massachusetts Historical Review* 6 (2004): 11-37.

Tygiel, Jules. "The Negro Leagues" *OAH Magazine of History* 7.1 (Summer 1992): 24-27.